Almost 500 Pages of Whining

(*Or Limerence, depending on your taste.)

The collected works of:

139 Pages of Pining

aka

The (Better) Book of Longing

...139, 2.

...139, 3.

By Brody McVittie

aka Tragedy in Training

aka Exhausting since 1980

aka The first Rockstar writer since Chaucer

aka The Patron Saint of Sometimes

Table of Contents

Part One: 139 Pages of Pining (2006-ish)

Book One: For the girl who's leaving

Waiting for me to step up and be a man.....21
Does this even make sense?......................22
The only Two Words that can stop me..........25
I suck!!!..26
Come visit me!...29
This One goes out to Girlfriend #17.........31
*Still less than the rest of me....................33
So you shift your weight, and it weighs on me..34
Counting Curls...37
The Patron Saint of Sometimes....................40
She's the type who tells you she doesn't like sad songs, right before she tells you it's over..42
'Leaving' is a four-letter word...................46
Things she says to me (in and around the things she says to me).........................47
The Latest Thing I Dislike About You........50

The Latest in a List of things I'll never
say to You..51
I don't even know what the fuck an
Ottoman is..53

'Failure' starts with my favorite
letter..56
Today's break-up is brought to you by the
letter 'G'..57
Exhausting Since 1980................................60

The Alchemy of Me........64

Before You leave (for the thousandth
fucking time)..66
5,368,232 words, for two......................68

Book 2: For the girl who's gone.

"..." 70
Of Going The Way You Go.................................71

Another over-elaborate way of saying something...........73

Normal, and other things I used to be.......76
Thank your lucky stars I'm not published..80
Of all the things I'm addicted to, you taste best..82
Baby, everybody has a talent or two..........83
Tuesday, for your information, is still cheap night..84
(More) Fun With Numbers.................................86

Ten digits deep...............87

B is for Burden..90
Me, and other things you left (when you left)..93

'Unfixable' is just a buzz-word for Broken...............94
June 19, 2006, and here you are......................95

Really, 'fire' is the only element we didn't lack...97
Sick, yeah, but with an 'l' in it (--so 'slick.')...99
Here's to War, and waging it........................103
Words we used To, For, Against & About one another...105
More of the things Time (and his friend Tequila) makes me miss...................................107
Intent vs. The Shit That Comes Out Of Your Mouth..110
The Sin of Something Else..........................114
'Promise' is a four-letter word...................116
Creative Uses of My Favorite Word............118
(Two things that don't necessarily go well together.)...120
Time, and other tiny tragedies...................121
Sightings and shit....................................123
Damn, if I don't sense a pattern.................125

I win............127

Similes, I guess............128
Twisting tongues and feelings............129
Second Place is for losers and
Indianapolis Colts............131
Take your jar of insecurities, and-............133
Names, and other things I called you............135
Day Four............139
Something clever I came up with, waiting
to not wait for you (anymore.)............143
Something you said, I guess, reminded me
of something Pa used to say............146
Grain............149
Today I spell sadness _ _ _ _ _
(A.I.M.E.E)............153
Gorillas and Ghosts............160
... Don't Worry Ma; It's A Metaphor............161
No further down............162
Things I Miss Most
(As Told By the Ten-Year-Old You Turned
Me Into)............165

Speaking of Analogies............166

Book 3: For the girl who's stupid enough to stay.

Close that fucking door-there's a draft coming in..168
You might be taking this the wrong way..170
Of Scars and Ones who Scarred Me............172
More buzzwords for broken.........................174
And you say I never write about you........176

Other couples say it's the cutest thing about us!..................178

Truths Rolled In And Around Ego...............179
What I've learned, after looking back at all of this...181

Part Two: ...139, 2. (2018)

The Ones to Get You

You walked into a room full of people....183
Older Indiscretions, Newer Consequences 184
More than mom likes whiskey........................187
Inappropriate...188
Okay, you win, but......................................190
Mehrabian's Rule..191
This one is about tattoos...kinda.................193
You'd look good in the passenger seat......195
...more than that toy when I was six........196
The one about that thing I got you for your birthday..197
The realest shit I've ever wrote.................198

Being sick as a kid sucks................................199

Always did like playing games..................200
Stairs, and shit...202
Seven Seasons..203
Protective...204
You're better to stay away........................205
Interlude..206

The Ones to Keep You

This section is decidedly smaller............208
7 & 7..209
7 & 9..210
You're Double-Stuffed Oreos......................213
Us, by the numbers......................................214
"Does this make my ass look fat?"..............215

Chicken Soup..216

Saturdays are for..217
Sundays are for..218
Your clothes on the floor...............................219
Favorite and Four-Letter Words..................220
I'm an acquired taste....................................221
I'm Bi-Polar, maybe..222
Hotel hallways, weak analogies...................223
You should have been a boxer.....................224
If relationships are like fights.......................225
I'm no good for you.......................................226
This will end violently....................................227
Pedestals are prisons...................................229
"Ten Things I Don't Deserve!"......................230
You're distractingly pretty and suitcase small..231
I guess that's why they call it the blues..233

I like spending time with you……………….234
What happens when wine…………………….235
Editors and English Teachers……………….236
You're four feet, one hundred miles away;………………………………………………….237

I like you more than sushi……………….238

Interlude………………………………………….239

The Ones to Lose You

For such a cute voice.................................242
I like you more.......................................243
You're on your way out the door..............244
Mine...245
Tiny Eventualities....................................246
I hurl words like weapons......................248
You woulda been perfect........................249
AZ..250
I'm fucking you.......................................252
I messed up...253
80 Pages in,...255
You're better than me.............................256
I'm losing you on rerun...........................257
Roses to Rust...258
Little Johnny Reiner................................259
Tell your parents.....................................260
I'm at least every cliché..........................261
because 'Gilbert' isn't a sexy town name...263
You don't fall..265
...in light of explanations, here's one that hurts..267
I create monsters....................................268
Weekends go by......................................269
I'll miss the nights..................................270
Here's a hint..271
I'm over...272
I wrote four of these...............................273

Patterns are for bad shirts..........................274
Losing you is the only thing worse..........275
I play with fire..276
Gambling isn't good to me............................277
As if..278
Yeah, you're the best I'll ever have..........279
I don't miss the hair......................................280
"Don't Let Me Push You Away"......................281

Saudade...282

Tell me..283
I'd rather..285
In your life..286
Today I almost threw out..............................287
In your defense..288
I thought about you once..............................289
Interlude..290

The Ones about Me

Of all the Irrational Animals,...................292
Inconsistently awful...........................293
I write volumes................................294
I've been writing more.........................295
I'm worse on the weekend.......................296
I need Jesus...................................298
Despair and Determination......................299
Irascible, but justifiably so..................300
Dressing pretty................................302
Motivation.....................................303
My Momma's Not Gonna Like This One.........304
I go for girls.................................305
I'm on my Marcus Aurelius shit.................306
I'm less about half-naked selfies............307
So can we call these lyrics?...................308
My Daddy isn't overly proud of me..........309
I'm suicidal before coffee.....................310
If my books are albums, then this shit is an EP...311
Friends and family members.....................312
138 Pages of Pining............................313
Last One.......................................314

Part Three: ...139, 3. (2019)

The Ones You're Likely Tired Of.

One about socks, and ruining them………..316
One about singing (...which I can't do.)…..317
One about time taking things…………………318
One about taking four pills(!)…………………321
One about Leo Season……………………………322
One about 2:38 on a Tuesday…………………324
One about downplaying Insecurities……..325
One about making shit up on the go……..326
One about where we come from …………328
One about Bon Iver…………………………………329
One about a pretty big dare…………………331
One about ten kinds of cancer………………332
One about Why, mom……………………………334
One about gushy love shit……………………335
One about Sentimentality………………………337
One more about math, which I hate…………338
One about your eyes……………………………339
One about what you can look forward to340
One about writing thirty-three pages(!).341

The Ones You Might Maybe Like.

You're more than those big green eyes....343
You look like Jesus, probably...................344
Burning gas and validation........................345
Prince of Lies-To..346
Eyes like honey, ass like.............................347
Whiskey and cocaine and other fun..........348
'Optimism' and other four-letter words..349
Whiskey on Wednesdays...............................350
Despite your obviously epic eyes/ass......351
There's a chance I'm gonna lose the toe...352
All burned out on bad behavior.................354
I'm not scared of monsters under..............355
My favorite word that starts with 'l'......356
You and those lips..357
Peanut Butter and Jam..................................359
You're kinda fancy...360
Troubadour, Fighting Man, Fool..................361
Static Cling..362
We're a match..363
Eating Disorders and Enthusiasm.............364
Heat Lightning and High Tops....................365
I Went Twelve Rounds with Chemistry......366
You've been on one since Bono....................367

The Ones I'll Likely Regret by the time This Comes Out.

Seriously..369
How much more 'that much better'..............370
Road Trips and Bad Days..............................371
Because Fuck Sleeping Dogs.........................372
Where I come from..373
This shit is so next level............................374
This One is '139 Pages of Pining, 3'...........375
Maybe the Next One......................................376
So there's blood in my urine.....................377
Mr. Missed the Mark...................................378
The One That Could Change My Life..........379

I'm Ten Kinds of Crazy..................380

Mitigate your Remembrance..........................381
The dichotomy being....................................382
Maybe the next one......................................383
I came up with ten pages............................384
How fucking cool..386
Horribly Self-Centered...............................387
This has to be like 80.................................388
Raggedy Rough Wild......................................389

The Ones I Can't Fit into Other Categories.

All of this is exhausting............................391
I took a break.......................................393
The grand total of my labors...................394
Table your transgressions.......................396
From the Jump......................................397
Exercise and Exorcise............................398
You kinda killed pizza on Fridays..........400
On some island/summer breeze shit...........401
Yes, my parents are disappointed.............402
Today's Sobering Cold Comfort..................404
Crushingly Insensitive..........................405
I (really) wrote 9 books about You............406
"It'll be better in the long run".............407
"Write One About Me".............................408
You're determined.................................409
I See Ghosts..410
Remember the time................................411
18 years of writing..............................412
Older just kinda means desperate..............413
Easy to read..414
I ran out of clever..............................415

The Ones That I hope are Kinda Clever.

You wear 'Hard to Get'..........................417
You put the gravel in my guts.................418
You always hated (thermostat shit)..........419
Here it is, the latest and greatest..........420
Wild(ly).......................................421
I'm like Trip Fontaine.........................422
Don't worry....................................423
I'm a fully confident sexed-up.................424
Climbing over clichés..........................426
How many more Really Fucking Clever....427
Remember all the times.........................428
Springfield, Ontario...........................429
The kind of not confident......................430
You're warm and cozy...........................431

Fuck you, do better..........................432

I mean, I've still got it......................433
I'm terrified of planes........................435
Running out of pages to write on..............437
I remember thinking there was so much..438
Confuse contemplation/commiseration....439
This is the home stretch.......................441
I can't remember...............................442
A big 'Thank You'..............................445

139 Pages of Pining

(aka The Better Book of Longing.)

Book 1: For the girl who's leaving.

...

Waiting for me to step up and be a man.

She turns to me, and she says

I can't live this way anymore.

So I look at her, and I say

Hold your breath, baby, and I'll get us out

And then I look away

and I hope to God

She's got the lung capacity.

...

Does this even make sense?

She says I'll never be good enough

in breaths and between

the breaths she breathes

away from me.

And she says she just

knows,

you know,

the way you know

when you look in the eyes of the one

you waited for;

waited for, for maybe just a little too long.

So I take the hit on the chin

like it came from Tyson

then;

on my way down

to the ground

she's grounding me on,

I'm thinking of ways

I'll pick myself back up.

But up is down

and I'm on the ground,

just the latest in a line

of lines she feeds me

in between the breaths she breathes

away from me.

...

The only Two Words that can stop me...

Let

and

Go.

...

I suck!!!

And you're the latest

in a line of things I've failed to conquer;

So congrats on being *elusive*,

like the high score in Donkey Kong

or

passing that Grade 10 math

or

anything, really, that has to do with loving

or

not-loving

the rest of you attached to that smile

and

those eyes

and

that ass.

And all I can really do

is reflect

and

wonder

what book I have to bury my head in

to finally be able to

make the grade

and

be the boy

that succeeds in really, really

really

breaking *you* down, too.

Come visit me!

I live

foot planted firmly in the past

At the cost of my present,

I know

And probably my future, too

if I fail at this

the way I am

The way I remain completely utterly unremarkable

on the off chance

that yourself or someone like you

reads this

And saves my life

the way I've been drowning and

trying to save yours.

...

This One goes out to Girlfriend #17.

I remember

the split-second I broke your heart;

some seconds south

of the time you looked at me

for the second time

with that

'I-told-you-so'

look;

telling me

without telling me

that breaking is all I'm really good at

and letting me down easy

some seconds south

of letting you down, too.

...

*Still less than the rest of me.

Okay, I should have gone after you

but chasing

is the opposite of running away;

and either

way

my feet hurt. *

So you shift your weight, and it weighs on me.

So you shift your weight

the way you do when you're sad

and it weighs on me

after you go the way you

go

when it hurts too bad.

Hurts, like that time in tenth grade

a girl named Summer left my heart

broken and bruised among Autumn leaves

she taught me the meaning of lives lived apart.

And the sting is back

in the back of my throat and somewhere south

watching you go the way you

go

already missing the taste in your mouth.

It moves, your mouth

on your way out the door

you shift your weight and you look over your shoulder

and you promise me

before you go

that it will ever and always sting more.

...

Counting Curls

She's got at least

two hundred and four

curls

that I count

while she sleeps

when she sleeps

beside me.

(--And *no*, you don't find that creepy.)

It's clever, more,

and it shows, kinda,

the kinda guy I was before;

the guy who could stay

awake and away

counting curls on her head

while she sleeps in my bed.

Now I'm watching

curls

walk out my door

and I'm sad again

just like

 before;

I lose another

left to wonder

how many more?

The Patron Saint of Sometimes

So I guess I'm

The Patron Saint of *Sometimes*;

Sometimes I'm good enough

Sometimes I'm man enough

Sometimes, she swears,

she might-*maybe* even love me.

Sometimes I work

out in the Wild and the Wind,

and Sometimes she says

the Wild's in me

and that's why she's *Gone With The;*

like that old movie

and Sometimes I wish

I wasn't running out of stairways

to call her back down from.

...

She's the type who tells you she doesn't like sad songs, right before she tells you it's over.

She's the kind

who's really just *not*.

She'll give you the eyes that say

stay

before pushing her lips to say

go away.

And she'll turn her head

just a little to the left;

and the look, you think, is just right

and you wonder where to take her next

and she's waiting for you to take her home

so she can tell you goodnight.

So you move closer

because it's time and you've put in the

 time

and she tells you it will take time

and much more

time

before the time you move your lips against

her lips

when she moves her lips

and not against yours

moves her lips to tell you

over dinner you're paying for

that it will take dinners

and many many more.

She's every sad song

on the radio on the way home;

and the curves in the road

have you picturing hers

the way you will tonight

alone.

...

'Leaving' is a four-letter word.

And it's still dark

and there's no light

and I toss and turn

'cuz we fuss and fight

and not for the ways

I wish I could say

That would make you stay

just one more day.

...

Things she says to me (in and around the things she says to me)

She says to me

in and around the things she says to me

that she grew up thinking men

were like the men

she grew up watching on TV.

Men like Kirk

comma Captain;

and men she grew up reading about

men like Captain

fucking America.

So she says to me

in and around the things she says to me

that I'm maybe half and *less*

the kind of man

she needs me to be.

And it hurts and more

than the fists that follow

the words that hit me

a half second and harder

than her fists and the look behind them;

the look that says

she's leaving,

leaving like the blood that runs

from the nose she breaks

not pumping her brakes

on her way out the door

to the next man

the next man

and his 'more.'

...

The Latest Thing I Dislike About You

Girls are supposed to be sweet

but you've got a mouth like a trucker

with a body that stops them,

truckers and the rest of traffic

trucking along in your Little Red Corvette

pumping Prince and the gas

on your way to somewhere

other than my place.

The Latest in a List of things I'll never say to You.

And there's a laundry list

of things I lack;

qualities, you'd say,

(if you spoke)

that make me less a man

more a monster;

but you don't

(speak)

but you do

(read)

so take in each and every word

I've ever written,

look me in my eyes

and tell me every last one of them

isn't

to

for

about

and

of

you.

I don't even know what the fuck an Ottoman is.

I'm on the ottoman

and Ambien™

and I'm thinking

--yeah, I really am-

about all the atrociously awful

extra crispy chicken shit

shit

you said to me

minutes before

you and your

minute little frame

bolted out my

door frame

taking pictures of us

framed or not

and putting them

where you put our love

somewhere lower than the shelves

we shelved our framed pictures

and inhibitions on

back when we decided

to share couches

with ridiculous names

...

'Failure' starts with my favorite letter.

She tells me I've failed

as a man.

I say,

Baby,

it's okay,

the only tests I ever flunked

were the ones that mattered anyway.

...

Today's break-up is brought to you by the letter 'G'

So come on use your words

cuz baby we're not that old

and there's still plenty of time

and plenty of lies

in our story

yet to be told.

So come on use your words

any which ones you choose

pretty words like leave and again and away

words that all mean

lose.

Like I will

when you use your word for last

time

and then the time comes far too fast

to hold you and stop you the way I

should;

hold you

and

stop you

the way

any real man would.

...

Exhausting Since 1980

She tells me I'm exhausting,

I say

Bitch!

I say

I've been Exhausting Since 1980.

I tell her I've trademarked that,

she tells me I've trademarked being the most unreasonable mess she's ever, ever messed with.

She tells me to

Beat It!

So I say

Bitch!

I say

I'm gonna beat it like Rihanna

should,

(and I mean beat it from the boy who beat her.)

And can you blame me?

I mean, I'm on tap to be

the first Rockstar Writer since Chaucer

(and I trademarked that, too, I tell her)

and she tells me

I'll amount to *less*

than the *half* a man

she tells me I am

before she tells me to

Beat It!

again.

So I just

Beat It!

Beat It!

right out that

Bitch!

's

door,

'cuz even though I'm not a

(lower case)

rockstar

yet,

I'm on tap to be bigger

than those before.

...

The Alchemy of Me

She tells me I take things

And I take it hard

And she tells me hard is how I take

the things I tend to take;

things like dreams and ambitions and futures

And she tells me these are the things I would realize

if I stopped to take the time;

She tells me all of this

And I just sit there and take it.

...

Before You leave (for the thousandth fucking time)

You can leave

and I won't stop you;

You can say

the things you'll say

about the boy I am

about the man I'm not

Things you used to say

to yourself in whispers

you can say louder now

before you go away

Just please, one last thing

before you say the things

you stayed to say;

look me in the eyes

and then

try

to walk away.

5,368,232 words, for two.

don't. go.

Book 2: For the girl who's gone.

"..."

You always said

the pain made the writing better;

congratulations,

today I'm fucking Shakespeare.

...

Of Going The Way You Go.

Writing is getting harder

and

not

writing is getting easier

and

any which way you look at it

you're gone;

and

this dream I had

of making a career of it

is well on its way

chasing you out my door.

...

Another over-elaborate way of saying something

There was something you said

once

and

without saying anything at all, really;

something said that stayed

long after you did;

something said, and sadly

with your eyes and the wild in them

and without your lips and the words between them;

something that sounded

sweetly

and in passing,

something like

'I-believe-in-you'

when no one else would or could or, I guess

even should;

so I just want you to know

that every word I ever wrote

and every word I ever will

is really just my round-about way of saying

something like

'Thanks.'

...

Normal, and other things I used to be

I used to have this sweater.

And I used to be normal, you know

Ten Fingers, Ten Toes.

I used to root for Jordan in the finals

and I used to tell myself,

'It's okay, tomorrow's another day'

I used to like ice cream

the way, I imagine, polar bears like snow days

I used to color outside the lines

and I used to want to

And then I met you

and then the things I used to want

I didn't want half as bad

as how bad-bad-I wanted you

So I used to have this sweater

And yeah, you know the one

You used to say it smelled like me

Hell, you used to want it to

Too, the way you wanted me

Not half as bad, apparently

as I wanted you

You took more than my sweater

But I suppose you figured that out

When you left me, down *and*

Left me to polar bears and snow days

And coloring outside of lines;

There's not many I wouldn't have crossed for you

If you'd given me time

And you can take that knowledge too

But please,

please

I'm begging you

--mail me back my fucking sweater.

...

Thank your lucky stars I'm not published.

'cuz you like to play it

close to the vest;

and you swear at me

when you see me

and you swear everywhere else

that you're over it;

telling me

'I'm over it'

but you lie

and it's in those eyes

swearing sweetly

You're only sometimes always on my mind

You're only sometimes always on my mind

You're only sometimes always on my mind.

...

Of all the things I'm addicted to, you taste best.

Better than the coke, and the booze

and

the pills and the girls

and the girls and the girls

I take and I drink and I take

to make myself

something *other* than

completely and utterly

fucked

without you.

Baby, everybody has a talent or two.

Well, excuse me

if

missing you

is the only thing

I've ever been

really, really

really

good at.

...

Tuesday, for your information, is still cheap night.

Memories are my favorite movies

'cuz our story got it right;

and if I still had the

right

to call or talk or text

I'd mention

maybe and in passing

that the days I pass through

don't mean half as much

muted and projected on some screen

sitting there and remembering

how we did it first, and better.

...

(More) Fun With Numbers

One thing you should know;

if I'm still three-quarters crazy

then that leaves a quarter talent—

—so the next time you're out

with him or **him** or, heaven forbid,

him—

remember that me at 75%

is better than 95% of him(s)

110% of the time.

...

Ten digits deep.

You should know

that every number I never dialed

on every night I should have known better

was yours and yours alone.

And you should know

that I can lift worlds across these shoulders

and hold them there

in the forever between phone calls.

But when it comes to finding the strength

to push the buttons that will bring you back

my hands shake and

my fingers fail.

And you should know

that it's no excuse and yet

it's my latest

And you should know

that when you rest the ear you listen with

on the pillow I'm not next to

that I'm still

so very sorry.

...

B is for Burden

And B

is what she

used to call me,

B-4

she walked out the door

B-cuz, she said, she couldn't stay any more.

And it's a little B-cuz

I'm so fucking poor

and a little B-cuz

there's holes

in my floor.

C

it'd be easy for me

to just call her a 'whore'

and pretend like

I don't love her no more,

but the truth is--

--the truth is-

--fuck it,

I'm out of words that rhyme.

Fuck her.

...

Me, and other things you left (when you left).

And all you couldn't stand
is all I ever wanted
And all you left behind
is all I'll ever have
So I guess you could say
'Linger' is my ALPHA-adjective
just another word
wasted on ears not yours
Alone (in company)
in the wake you left
when you went the way you went,
SO...

...

'Unfixable' is just a buzz-word for Broken.

And broken is how you left me
And broken is all I am
Like that toy in the toy chest
I loved just NORTH
of really, really loving you
He-Man is unfixable
And I'm unfixable, too
Unfixable
Unfixable
Unfixable
Ever chasing after
You.

...

June 19, 2006, and here you are.

I STILL, just so you know.

Still seven digits, odds and evens, if you're interested.

Still breathe a little faster, a step slower—for the record, heart still stops.*

(*Almost forgot, in the time since, just how much that hurts.)

Still wake up,

same side, same bed,

pictures bleeding out of my head

Technicolor red,

trailing the green of the same toothpaste

down the drain of the place you run from.

Pictures of days feeling less like
memories, more like SOMETHING ELSE.

Still, though, six years removed.

Still relate the song on the radio to
the smile on that Thursday,
a Thursday less a memory.

You remember, still, standing there, or
are the feelings written on your face
for the tall, dark, and handsome guy
over my shoulder?

You still, just so you know.

Still smell cinnamon sugar, hibiscus,
and soul-ten manicured toes, and all
that.
Still look like the first day,
the day after
and days since.

Still...

Really, 'fire' is the only element we didn't lack.

And the fuel we used

to light the fires

we'd fight

when we'd fight

fires, *and*

can't compare

to the fuel

I find

looking back at

pictures of you

in and amongst the ash and the wreckage

we called our relationship.

...

Sick, yeah, but with an 'l' in it (--so 'slick.')

Well baby,

if my words

have pain in and around them

then my voice

has ten kinds of cancer.

And you call yours

Mike,

because he never calls

when he says he'll call.

And you call yours

Ken,

because he *left* you

when you needed him

to go the *other* direction.

But when I call

my voice needs chemo

and my words

are sicker still;

spoken in tongues

better suited

for tickling yours.

Before, after and around

leaving my name

all over your

tongue,

having tasted ten

still yearning for the sick

my voice still carries

on the tip-

--pushing words and pain

through teeth

better suited

for fumbling with your

tongue and

teeth between.

...

Here's to War, and waging it.

And you lied when you said

that my wounds would mend

And you lied when you swore

you'd be back for me someday

You should know, I wasn't lying

when I said the wars I've waged

in your name and wake

number in the thousand thousands;

And you should know, I wasn't lying

when I swore to wage

a thousand thousand more.

...

Words we used To, For, Against & About one another

I used the word

stay

three-thousand, four-hundred twenty-two and a half

times,

in the three-thousand, four-hundred twenty-two and a half

fights we fought;

apparently,

I should have used it

once

more.

...

More of the things Time (and his friend Tequila) makes me miss.

I miss writing

and

Thundercats on Saturday mornings.

I miss something for nothing

and

that feeling I used to feel

when I felt I was doing something

maybe

worth doing.

I miss my hairline,

and

that quarter I lost under some couch somewhere.

Yeah, for the thousand-thousandth time,

I miss you;

but

I don't miss you

half as much

as I motherfucking

miss *me*.

...

Intent vs. The Shit That Comes Out Of Your Mouth.

You say

with your mouth and your hips and your finger and *all that ass*

that I'm not

good enough and strong enough and smart enough and

(goddamn it)

good looking enough.

You say

with your actions and your intent and your scent and your

lack of

common sense

that I'm lacking in the qualities and the compassion and the comprehension

and the...

well, the *something else* you say I don't have,

in and amongst the things you're saying;

and I'm looking into your eyes

and trying not to smile

and *not* saying

(--because, despite what you say, I'm smarter than that--)

that you can go on and

say

all the things I'm not.

Your eyes say something else,

something that makes me smile,

say,

Yeah,

I love you, too.

...

The Sin of Something Else.

If I've written a thousand thousand words

then I've written

a thousand thousand words

for you.

If I've broken a hundred hundred hearts

then I've broken

a hundred hundred hearts

because you broke mine.

And if I could trade a million million nights

to go back to that one

Then I'd look in your eyes

and save them all.

I'd tell you I love you

the way I've been trying to,

Every word and heart broken

in the million million nights

since the night

I said something else instead.

...

'Promise' is a four-letter word.

I promise

I've broken

more than my share.

I promise

I'm nowhere closer

to close enough.

I promise

you can write it on my tombstone

Because I promise

somewhere beneath it

or somewhere above it

I'm thinking of you.

...

Creative Uses of My Favorite Word

Fuck I look good

without a shirt.

And fuck if I haven't

fucked my fair share

But fuck if I'm not

just fucking fucked

For fucking it up

the way I fucked it up

with you.

...

(Two things that don't necessarily go well together.)

We don't get along

cats and vacuum cleaners

and the home we built

is a six-by-nine with bars

but the bar I found you in

is the bar I left you in

and the bars we skipped between

meant something more than the nothing

nights without you

left me to

when you left me, too.

Time, and other tiny tragedies.

I'm still me

and

You're still you;

It's just time

that's tried to take

the memories and moments

but time

is just one more thing

that couldn't come close

and

time

is just one more thing

that can fuck right off.

...

Sightings and shit

So I saw you the other day

You were walking the other way

So away

and walking

You caught me watching

the way you walk

when you walk the only way

you've walked since

you went away

the way you've walked

since I said

stay.

...

Damn, if I don't sense a pattern

And damn if I don't remember

that afternoon some September

You came into my memory

And my mind

catching eyes and

thoughts

and the thoughts that follow

the eyes that follow you

absorbing your scent

and intent

on your way across

from me

and into me

and my memory;

walking my way

and then away

taking September

everywhere but with you

and

leaving me to my memories

of how much I miss you.

I win.

Kiss me
Tell me
Fuck me
Maim me

Twist me
Make me
Leave me
Break me

Still can't

Shake me.

...

Similes, I guess

When it comes to this writing shit

I'm colder than you're step-father.

Twisting tongues and feelings.

You manage to know

One hurt me so;

I dwell

as days go by

And you wonder why

I never reply

Just kind of sigh

It's like,

you say

I won't even try.

I hurt some too, you know

You remind me so

The lists in your mind

following words just unkind.

But lists are for groceries,

and some were just mean;

I dwell on a few

--leaving hurt girls--

to memories,

and cracks in between.

...

Second Place is for losers and Indianapolis Colts.

I used to call you

And

I used to call you 'sugartits' when I called you;

And

your new man calls you

And your new man calls you 'princess' when he calls you

So that's the difference between us

(well, that and the penis)

So settle for second

and count them too;

until you see me across some bar

and

realize that, no, second just won't do.

...

Take your jar of insecurities, and-

Hold your insecurities

up to the light

I bet you've got enough

to fill a jar.

Go on, fill it up

be sure to twist that lid tight,

you wouldn't want any to escape.

Take your jar full of insecurities

and put it up on the shelf

between your bottle of dreams

and your flask

of tiny little infidelities.

...

Names, and other things I called you

I can't take back

The words I said or

The names I called you or

The feelings you felt

because

I called you;

but if you could

remember

the first time

I called you

The way you felt

then

is the way I feel

now and still;

And if you'd

call

I think you'd find

my words

on the other end

said

maybe just a little

more sweetly

in between

Sorry

might hide names like

baby

right before

and again around

the words I'll say

when I say

Come home.

...

Day Four

So they say

it takes fourteen days

to kick a habit.

Here's day four

(hundred and more)

and kicking

memories of you

is harder than

the habits I kicked

to hold you

and down

like we used to be.

I can honestly say

I'd rather kick coke

the highs were less

the lows much more

watching and waiting

behind closed doors.

Steroids, I could go without

knowing no matter the size

knowing no matter the swell

I'll always feel small

here in this hell.

Heroin, they say,

laughs at fourteen;

well, Heroin never spent the night

in your sheets and your eyes

kissing the magic I'll miss

in between your thighs.

I took a handful

of Vicodin;

washed it down

with Ambien

couldn't drown

while drowning

flashes of my front door

and the sunlight that followed

you through on days

before you were through with me

...

Something clever I came up with, waiting to not wait for you (anymore.)

There are reasons

she does

--*reasons*, that is-

--reasons I'll never be

the kind of man

I would need to be

for her

to need me.

And,

she reasons

that reason

left me

some season

south of the season

she's leaving me

in

 and

  to;

some season

that feels a fuck of a lot like Winter

looking for reasons

she left,

like seasons

worth living in.

...

Something you said, I guess, reminded me of something Pa used to say

Pa used to say

good girls are like cars

you have to warm them up

before you turn them over

And it's the word of the day

over

like over you

and

not really at all

and

still,

which, really, might be tomorrow's word

if tonight stays

still

the way nights since

tend to do

every night

since that last

night

with

you.

Fucker.

...

Grain.

Let's say I put a grain of sand in a bucket

for every day

since the day

You

left

me.

Mondays and many

means grain and plenty.

One for each day at the window we shared,

looking past the night

until the sun makes it right

another grain and

a Tuesday to follow

another grain and

a little more hollow.

Not the pail, you see

the hollow's in me

The pail's just fine

with the passage of time.

A Wednesday and

a Sunday

and

a grain and a grain

and

again.

Looking out instead of in

for reasons you left me

with buckets of tin.

Words said for Wednesdays

sins are for Sundays

analyzing my dreams

I save for Mondays.

Until the Monday

or the Sunday

you come back to stay-

--all I have left

are things left to say.

That,

and this heavy fucking pail.

Today I spell sadness _ _ _ _

(A.I.M.E.E)

And she's sitting across from me,

A.I.M.E.E

and she's

All I May Ever Ever

want

and she's

All I May Ever Ever

need.

And sitting across from her

my eyes say

I want to devour you

and her eyes have

I could run circles around you

written in the circles

the dark of her mascara makes

when she smiles at me,

that

All I May Ever Ever

smile,

bats those

blue

blue

eyes,

breaks my heart clean in two.

So today I spell sadness

A.I.M.E.E

because spelling with those letters

doesn't spell the name of the one

waiting at home

for me to not be

sitting across

from A.I.M.E.E.

And no matter how many ways

I say and spell

words like

I would never do to you

what I'm doing to her,

A.I.M.E.E

and her

blue

blue

eyes

tell me they don't believe me,

don't believe me

because they really, really can't.

And so today I spell sadness

--and she knows the rest-

because I'll never taste

the cotton-candy lip-glossed

cotton candy of her lips

the way I really, really want to.

And the way

the

blue

of her

blue

blue

eyes tells me

she really, really wants me to

too,

knowing that it's wrong and completely

and

impossible and totally.

And today I spell sadness,

right after I spell goodbye

because A.I.M.E.E is leaving

me to memories of tables

and her across from them

one more thing between us

wrong

and

impossible

and

any way you spell it.

...

Gorillas and Ghosts.

I live on a farm

between gorillas and ghosts.

Ghosts in my head

gorillas in bed

and the ghosts are gorillas

in weight and the way they

weigh on my mind

there in my bed

next to tonight's gorilla

wishing I was beside

a ghost instead.

... Don't Worry Ma; It's A Metaphor

Thoughts of you are razors

across metaphorical wrists.

Yeah, I know it's dark

but you got the light

when you took half,

and all I kept

was your fucking cat.

...

No further down

How many years

have I wasted

remembering the ten seconds it took

for you to take

my breath and my

heart

and the rest of the half-life

you left me with

when you left me

how many years

ago.

Ten seconds

ten years on

years spent

with the seconds in them

second guessing

the mistake

ten seconds in the making

I made

when I made the choice

ten seconds or ten years

ago;

the choice to let you go;

let you go

knowing I was

nowhere near

man enough

to let you

stay for the seconds

ten, or however many it took

to save years

and my half-life

years on and

no further down the road

you walked away on.

Things I Miss Most

(As Told By the Ten-Year-Old You Turned Me Into)

-your red Skittles smile

-whole football quarters lost beneath covers

-the shampoo I never had the balls to buy on my own

-Everything.

Speaking of Analogies...

I left a light on.

Book 3: For the girl who's stupid enough to stay.

Close that fucking door—there's a draft coming in.

You have to understand,

there's things I miss

and things I don't.

There's places I'll let you take me

places I won't.

Times when I'll feel close to you

others...

sorry, I won't.

So please understand

I'll give you what's left,

closer to half

on account of the hole

the one the One left

when she left out the door.

Please, close it behind you

before asking for more.

...

You might be taking this the wrong way.

Compliments, to you, are four-letter words

'beautiful' is 'fat'

'lovely' is 'ugly'

and

if you could only see

the look on your face when I

mouth the words

to get you to open yours

around the parts of me you excite most;

And I swear it's exciting

when you swear back

in between words better suited, like

'leave' and you will

and

'fuck you'

like you really, really should.

Of Scars and Ones who Scarred Me.

All I've got

are my scars and the stories

my scars could tell you

of the Ones who scarred me.

There's Ones who smiled

and cut anyway

Ones who warned me they would

and surprised me the same

One who promised they couldn't

as the first knife sunk in

and One who shouldn't

because she was kin.

...

More buzzwords for broken.

'Clarity' can join 'comfort'

in my little list of words

that mean next to nothing

to my writing

and my relationships.

And

you tell me

my relationship to my writing

is clearly taking

the comfort from us—

--I tell you

--and I'll put it in writing

that 'us' is just ' me'

and

whatever patience I retain today.

...

And you say I never write about you.

If your name was a color

I'd swear it was my favorite

I might not mention it

but your lips are my favorite, too

I'll never say it

but I think about you

often and only when you're not around;

so the next time you are

around

cross your fingers and find

my arms and my lips

around yours

and

again

and

for real, this time.

...

Other couples say it's the cutest thing about us!

...

I wear haunted

Like you wear perfume

(so A LOT)

And I'm fine with it

The way you're REALLY, REALLY NOT

Because you're all I've got

And you've yet to realize you could do better.

...

Truths Rolled In And Around Ego.

You always said

my conscience lived

somewhere *south* of my smile;

and it's that

smile

and things south

that keep you coming

and back;

and on yours

and scratching and clawing

mine,

you swear to me

and

at me

that back is where you'll stay.

Epilogue:

What I've learned, after looking back at all of this...

Fuck.

I really need to get over you.

...139, 2.

139 Pages of Pining 2

The Ones to Get You

You walked into a room full of people

looked at me last

with a look that said you put me first

--so I blame the entirety of the following, in spirit if not historical fact

on you and your instigating little eyeballs.

Older Indiscretions, Newer Consequences

Sorry if I'm aggressive
Bully on a Grade Six playground

Maybe you bring out the worse
aspects of an already for-wear
personality

But you have to understand
being around you is two-dollar steak

So tough

Like that math test back then
that made recess so volatile

Hiding anxieties and marbles

Stolen like the kisses I'm trying to

Too many years, and no better off.
I'm tired of counting colors in eyes
just north of lips I can't taste

Watching you and wanting
you watching and wanting, too

Wasting wonderfully
running out of time and the chances time
both brings and takes

Taking it out on each other with words
better saved
Spoken loudly from mouths
better suited

For anything other than the everything we're spending all our wasted time

not doing.

I like you

more than mom likes whiskey.

Inappropriate

Is what you call me

And us

And my intentions

Throwing words into your coffee cup

Swallowing blonde roast and the words you won't

Invitation

And please

And more

Hanging your head on circumstance and
mistrust and other adjectives that matter
as much as the rest of the words you don't
speak when your lips are busy against
mine and between sips that only taste half
as good.

Okay, you win, but....

So I can't get your number

And I can't get you to stay

And I can't get you to admit what we both already know is true

You tell me I can't have it all

Or anything, at all

So can you please, do me one kindness before you go

Pick up this book, and point to a word that you don't feel

A verse you can't understand

A line that isn't about you.

Mehrabian's Rule

My boy Albert famously said

Only <u>seven percent</u> of communication is verbal

--and I'm thankful, because that's the part you suck at

Wasting words like "shouldn't" and "can't" and "fuck, I'd never trust you"

He tells me <u>thirty-eight percent</u> is voice and tone

--and I'm thankful, because you're good at that

Flirtations in whispers and acknowledgements, like "yes, under different circumstances"

But the part you kill

is the *fifty-five percent* body language

Speaking in tongues and fluently

Punching with pheromones and frequently

Telling me without telling me

What my boy Albert already knows

That, despite your thinly-veiled resistance

Us

Is a matter of time

and

Only.

*This one is about tattoos
...kinda.*

...but it's really about you, too.

There's room on my sleeve

(--not much)

For you to scar me permanently the way

you kinda already have

Looking like you look and leaving like you

Leave

And me to nights with nothing but the stories tattooed onto my arms

Holding whiskey instead of

And hoping the pen can scratch something

Worth the needle I'd let you hold

Leaving something that promises to

Stay

A little longer than you tend to.

You'd look good in the passenger seat

Stealing away to some/anywhere

Away from the here I'm chained to and you're young enough to believe you're not and maybe might not be

And

You're the kind I'd even let control the music

Relinquishing more than I'd like to

Adding miles to the too many I've got

Taking my eyes off the road and figuring maybe I've got one last story to tell

Lost on some back road

The way we've been trying to

...more than that toy when I was six.

I want you more

than that toy when I was six.

The one that I prayed for

to a God I haven't believed in

since that prayer came true.

And if I only get one,

I'll go back and tell that six year old

hold off on that toy

the next one you want

more than anything in the whole wide world

will be worth the next thirty-one years without.

The one about that thing I got you for your birthday

You wanted a knife for your birthday

--because you're that kind of girl and why not

and because it's not the kind of thing you'd ask the person you pretend to love for

--because he's not that kind of guy and can't be.

So the gifts with the ability to cut come from me

and maybe it's metaphor for the kind of thing we have and can't help

danger on edges, black polished steel and engravings

carved into surfaces, setting something in steel

and as real as the blood from that first cut.

The realest shit I've ever wrote

is the shit I've yet to write about you.

Being sick as a kid sucks.

I came into this world ugly

And so I handle things the same

And meningitis couldn't kill me

The way that girl tried back then

So it's ugly but it works, somehow

And I'm still here

Although I apologize for the way this starts

I can try my damndest to see it doesn't end that way

If you'll wait me out

The way catastrophic childhood diseases

And homicidal exes couldn't.

Always did like playing games

You're my latest last chance at being happy

So congrats on that

The new Super Mario Bros. when I was seven

The new boobs at fifteen

First house at twenty-three

And I'm older, yeah, but I still have one more run

Towards and not the other way

Because being happy is more important

Than being successful or well-off or even doing well

Being happy is all I've got left to chase

And so

tag,

you're it.

Stairs, and shit.

You're at the top of a staircase

And not just metaphorically

And you're not supposed to be calling me to you

The way you're calling me to you

So I'm climbing stairs

Literally

Overcoming all of your tiny resistances with every step

Hoping the top is worth the work

Wearing out the soles of shoes

Better suited for the way down

That's waiting on the other side of you.

Seven Seasons

You smell like hibiscus

and other things that are fun to say and hard to spell

easily in the *'Top Three Most Enticing Things About You!'*

right under

your eyes

and

everything ;

and in the taking in and the tasting of

hidden behind doors with way too many windows

I'm wondering if unplanned intrusions or

buildings on fire

could pull me away from seven seasons worth of waiting

frustrations taken out on lips that taste as good as they've looked

for as long as I've looked at them.

Protective

is the adjective you like to hang on,

Like of your feelings and your heart and all of the other things you claim I'm intent on taking

And you're right

about the taking if not the need

For the word you use to describe the excuses you tell yourself

Warding off advances and eventualities

Putting up a fight better saved

For the tangling coming after

You hang up your favorite word

And relent to one

just

like

this.

You're better to stay away

because it would be six Saturdays before I'd let you out of the war

we'd call bed

Scratching and clawing and entangling

for all the scratching and clawing and entangling

it took to land us to land between sheets in the first place

So please, for the sake of peace and prosperity

ignore the loaded guns I call longing glances

save your grenades for boys as half-beautiful;

Stick to the wars you're equipped to win.

Interlude

I'm at this book signing

Signing books that are better

Than the books I'm surrounded by;

Books about poetry,

Because poetry is hot right now

But not as hot as mine

And I'm going to write

...139, 2

To prove it to you

And the rest of the world

And I'm sorry

It'll take me tearing you apart

for 139 Pages, too

To prove it.

The Ones to Keep You

This section is decidedly smaller

By design and degrees;

Because no one reads a book called

"139 Pages of Pining"

For happy shit.

7 & 7

You're Seagram's and 7-Up

Cocaine and Coffee

...pretty much everything that tastes good and is better for you.

7 & 9

are numbers and initials

and initially

that's all they were and could be;

Circumstances and other terrible words that start with consonants keeping the eventuality of

Us

somewhere other than

right here

and

right now

and

right here

and

right now

I'm looking down at the arm with your initial scratched on it

And I'm pretty fucking thankful

my initial on your little foot

is being scratched on too;

Circumstances going the way of complications that start with consonants

And leaving eventualities and hidden meanings to start and stay

the way that tattoo needle promises they will.

You're Double-Stuffed Oreos

to my inner fat kid;

90 mile per hour run from the cops

to my socially-challenged/misunderstood mid-twenties

Heroin

to my just-wait-till-I'm-successful indulgencies

Yeah, I guess this is my way of saying

You're pretty

and pretty cool.

Us, by the numbers

I'm 67% schizophrenic

(--and I have the brain scan to prove it)

23% righteous anger

and whatever's left

is the space to like

Someone like You;

99% Pure like that soap claims to be

1% crazy as fuck

for liking me, too.

"Does this make my ass look fat?"

And the answer is

Yes,

And thank-the-God-I-Don't-Believe-in for it,

Because it's 2018

And baby, your fat ass is, to the eloquent gentleman in me

My Favorite thing about you.

So park it in the passenger seat

And hold on tight;

Despite what everything you've ever read about me has told you,

I swear this won't end the bad my fifty-thousand-four-hundred-Sixty-two words printed would beg to differ.

Chicken Soup

ain't got shit on you.

Saturdays are for

Curling on couches

(--outside of football season)

Movie marathons and

Red wine

and

Light sodomy;

and

Driving to destinations

Far away from here and the reality

We want no part of

But spend the majority of days ending in 'y' tethered to.

Sundays are for driving

(--outside of football season)

and back from whatever destination we ran away to;

back to the reality of shared workplaces and the secrets we're forced to keep

pent up, round pen,

Horses

let loose on Fridays

Power pushing us down roads

and away from the reality/predicament we find ourselves in.

Your clothes on the floor

Comfort in ways

The blankets we tangle in

Never could;

The only mess my self-diagnosed OCD can justify

They're a mess

And yet

Less

Than the mess I'll make of

You

Covered in tangled sheets and the mess my love makes

All over you and yet not

The clothes you'll escape in.

Favorite and Four-Letter Words

Stay

and

Next,

respectively.

I'm an acquired taste

admittedly,

Beer to a ten-year-old

Broken wing to a Ballerina,

the kind of maybe-not-sure

that told you to stay away

and got you into this mess,

equal parts

"maybe it's not so bad"

and

"fuck I need to leave."

I'm Bi-Polar, maybe

Most likely when it comes to the ball of yarn in my head

Most certainly when it comes to processing

Anything that has to do with you

And that smile

And that ass;

Like I need/want/can't-stand-it

Around or over you

So while I apologize for the drama that comes

With dating me

I don't apologize

--get it?

Hotel hallways, weak analogies

I was raised in hotel hallways

More out there than in here

And I'm always sleeping outside

Missing out on the conversations and the kinds of things I suppose one

conventionally keeps behind closed doors

So why not out in the open anyways

If all the world is a stage

And we all have our parts to play

Let me show you what you've been missing

Hiding away under pesky ceilings.

You should have been a boxer.

you move faster

and you hit harder

tip-toeing around the rings we spar in

throwing words and hooks and jabs

and even though you're punching above your weight class

you're winning every round

I'm running out of canvas to circle

before you put me down.

If relationships are like fights

then I've won more than I've lost

(--fuck it, I am a fighter, and I've won more than I've lost)

But I know full well
I'm going to take an L with you

worth the beating and the bruising and the scratching and the blood

black eyes and sore teeth and scarred skin and light head

still swinging for proverbial fences

still pursing for literal kisses

because concussions are fun

and your taste twice as.

I'm no good for you

is today's understatement of the year,

compounded and kissed by the simple fact that I want you too much to lose you

the way we both know I already kinda *am*,

three weeks into something that carries

the weight of seasons comma seven

And I've placed burdens on shoulders slim as yours

for the totality of the time I've tricked

girls as half-beautiful as you

into believing I'm actually the guy you see on the poster

less 'as advertised' and more 'hazard: dangerous road ahead.'

This will end violently

Because that's how it goes

and

Because I guess we've kinda earned it;

Down in flames the way

the great ones always go

Left scarred and fuck that second r

so

scared

And of opening as wide and burning as bad

as skinned knees at seven

But not healing half as well

Thirty years and several layers removed

Going down swinging

For what I hope is the last time,

Running out of flesh left to tear.

Pedestals are Prisons.

just another name,

like 'King of Pop'

for Mike;

Bad

but undeniable just the same.

So I'm still about the placings

(--in case you bothered to read the first one)

but I'm getting better at recognizing the bars pedestals and my placings-on are presenting in patterns,

stripes on shirts I'd prefer stay solid.

You're right at the top,

"Ten Things I Don't Deserve!"

but take anyways,

right above

Skittles from my baby sister when she was seven

and

Everything,

leaving you with nothing

save the promises I break when I promise I'm worth the love I've spent considerable time taking.

You're distractingly pretty and suitcase small

Too pretty for pieces,

which is why the protector in me

prefers you stay in situations, safe

So stay

because it's late and I've got knives

and I promise you're safer here

than the *anywhere out there*

I'll tell you just about anything

to keep you from.

...

Yeah, the danger's more

Out there

than

In here

and when you look into my eyes

the fact that you believe

makes you the victim we both kinda understand you're about to be.

I guess that's why they call it the blues

Said somebody much better at this than me,

And I only see red on days without you in them

So consider time spent charity

Medicine for a breaking, slowly soul

And keep the prescription on refill,

because running out is a crawl to crimson

And I'm dead out of anything but you.

I like spending time with You

is code

for something much more

something that starts with

I

and ends in

You

and, just so you know...

...I like spending time with You, too.

What happens when wine

doesn't taste as good when it's not together?

Editors and English Teachers loved me

Mothers and Fathers, not so much

And you'll end up somewhere in the middle

After the first words about you

Bleed into the ones after

Once you realize the honey

Stops at honeyed words

And that the guy writing them

Presents well and preserves poorly.

You're four feet, one hundred miles away;

Head down and typing furiously on a phone better suited for sending furiously typed texts to me

Sending someone else the somethings I've been missing

So please, put away the distractions

you pretend to distract yourself with,

Focus on the features that landed you in trouble in the first place

and acknowledge that spelling out the things I'm not can't fill

me and the holes my personality punched.

I like you more than sushi

--so a whole fucking lot

And I need you more than

-corrective eye surgery

-rehab

-Jesus

And the litany of things my doctor and my mother tell me I need;

taking the lead with big eyes and big hair and that ass,

Priority Number One, even on the nights the whiskey and my rampant alcoholism beg to differ.

Interlude

I'm horrible at the following;

-paying attention

-math

-dancing

-adult life

-you

However, one of the two things I'm good at

Is writing *this*,

and this shit is popular now

Bookstores full of poetry books that absolutely fucking suck

but are more popular

So do me a favor

Tell your friends this one is about you

--because it kinda is

--and tell your friends to pick up a copy

Because it's Better than the shit they're reading, too.

The Ones to Lose You

For such a cute voice

you sure make hurtful sounds.

I like you more

than the things I really like

Cocaine

and

Coffee

and

the other wonderful things that come from

the magical made-up land you come from

And I'll write my next-best book about it

So stay tuned

In the meantime

Here's to the hurt I'm about to

Blowing this because I tend to

Having read the end to the book I'll write about you.

You're on your way out the door

Literally

and

Figuratively

and I figure

it's for the best

Because I pushed you here

and

I'm

too tired/stubborn/stupid

to admit that this may be the first of

what admittedly might be

a Season of bad ideas.

Mine

and

Stay

are the most powerful words in the
English language.

And they hate each other

because they know they *can't*

make you do either or be,

Gone

and

Long

left and pretty fucking powerful, too.

Tiny Eventualities.

I always kinda figured I'd end up here

Prison, real or imagined

Stealing cars and hearts

for far too many years to get away with it

the way I was until you

Put me here

And the bars might be metaphorical or they might not be metaphorical

but no better off

having known we both saw this coming

and couldn't end up anywhere than

here

and where you leave me

the way you should

to the cage I knew I'd find

not quite the man it takes to avoid tiny eventualities.

I hurl words like weapons

because yours hurt too,

marriage

and

kids

daggers, parried with

single

and

never

the words that won the war

and left me the alone

that maybe this book and these words kinda make me have to be.

You woulda been perfect

a partner and a pal and a shoulder and a soul

but

perfect isn't quite the ending I figured I deserve

and so

I had to sell you short

like the short I said I fell in love with

five-foot-nothing and standing taller now,

the all alone I freed you to.

AZ

You're 3,475 miles away
literally,
and maybe double that
leaving things the way we leave them.

And still I figure
you're the best/worst thing for me

black hair and blue eyes
leaving me the kinda colors

you backing off
has beat me down to.

So I'll love you from the distance
the miles were kind enough to create

settle for the knowing

that proximity is poison

when two people exchange particles

with the fury and the fire

we exchanged ours.

And yeah, I love you

and yeah, I always will

but you should stay in your corner

warm and dry and safe

and leave the winter and the cold

to someone better suited

for the black fingers and blue toes

your winter wake wound up wounding when you left.

I'm fucking you

And over

And you're doing your best to stay the pretty that got you into trouble in the first place,

Finishing somewhere other than the

First place

I promised when I lied,

First of several you put up a good fight fighting

Right before the fucking

--and over!

began.

I guess you could say

"I messed up"

is an oversimplification, *kinda*

Like saying that

turning out to really be

everything I said

foreshadowed

promised

I was and am

is a surprise.

So

Surprise!

I'm an asshole and a liar and a bamboozler

--and not just because it's my favorite word

but because I promise I'm the same hopeless case

I was when I promised

and you made the mistake of loving me anyways.

80 Pages in,

and I'm running out of steam;

and it's not like

I haven't hurt the 59 women I need to have hurt

To fill the rest of the pages I promised;

but fuck if writing down my celebrated list of failures

hasn't left me a little uninspired

--so heaven forgive the next number I call

In the name of finishing this book

Sorry in advance

for the next page

--the first of a few

likely about you.

You're better than me

at math and polite conversation and at *this*

--the whole 'love' thing

and maybe it's because of this that I string you along,

pretending really hard, (because that's all I've ever been really good at)

when I look you in the eyes and promise that

No

I won't hurt you again and

No

I'm not hurting you right now

Latest in a series of lies I might maybe lie myself into believing.

I'm losing you on rerun

--meaning I've seen this movie before;

and pressing pause won't change the ending

So spoiler alert(!)

the car crash is coming

and you're going to be left a little worse for wear

wearing that t-shirt I gave you

on the first Wednesday since the wreckage

telling yourself that having your name in the credits

means you'll be remembered when the screen goes black.

Roses to Rust

I'll turn roses to rust

On my 'left out in the rain' shit

real good at ruining

pretty little things like you

and writing clever words about it

After the hurt has gone

the way of the pedals

put down on to the floor

of the cute little cars

You and the other ones run away in.

Little Johnny Reiner

I lost a fight in the seventh grade

when Johnny Reiner kicked me in the balls

--and this kinda feels like that,

laying on the playground and praying

that my poor little grade seven balls grow back

After the metaphorical kicking

your up and leaving

has left me laying in.

Tell your parents

And your dignity

And your goddamned dog

And our unborn child

And your Saturday night complacencies

I'm sorry

For the future(s) I've freed

And you're welcome

For the renewed patience

And restored sanity.

I'm at least every cliché

You're right about that,

and

'Danger'

tattooed on my forehead

is about the only tattoo I don't have;

Covering up tiny insecurities and superficial flaws

with tiny little cartoon angels and demons

to represent the saving I need and the
devil I am

Coming as advertised when that tiny
little voice tells you

Runaway

the way these words are trying to.

...because 'Gilbert' isn't a sexy town name.

You're close to Tempe,
One 'r' short of
Temper

--close to describing you too,
and how you react to my inability to
act on the promises I promised you.

And maybe I was too scared to tell you

You scare me

At least twice as beautiful

As the beautiful I'm used to

Three hours behind

Bit ahead in absolutely everything else

Already realizing you've got the potential

To get the best of me,

Hiding up North and under blankets

Ruining the chance to ruin my bed

And the blankets I could have been under with you, too.

You don't fall

back or forward

down there;

So if Daylight Savings Time can't fool you

what chance did a fool like me have

You saw right through

the me I tried to be

because I really really wanted to;

Focused instead on the man I am

maybe more importantly,

The man I'm not

So I see you're happy

and I am, for you

Way up here, three or four ahead

depending on the season

Some seasons since you failed to fall for me.

...in light of explanations, here's one that hurts

I aged better than most of the girls in the books I wrote.

And it's about the only thing I'm not sorry for

Because if you spent any kinda time with me

You were fair game

for the words I wrote to wash off the sins I probably sinned but blamed

any-all of you temporarily foolish enough to stay

And eventually smart enough to leave

me and the pages I probably wrote to get back at you.

I create monsters

and then cut them loose.

Weekends go by

And you're anywhere else

and tonight's a Saturday

and that same bar is holding you down

the way I used to;

So while you're collecting attention

I'm catching the kinds of feels

it takes to write this,

One more page

Until I'm both done and famous

and everywhere else

But that same bar

That'll still be holding you down.

I'll miss the nights

with just you in them;

the ones with wine

and wasted time

the ones with drugs

and the sleep drugs bring

holding you

way back when

the only thing we missed

was the alarm in the morning

and ruined

was just the sheets.

Here's a hint;

When I say

"I'm fine"

I'm really

really

Not

and

the way your breath stops

when you walk away

--just that little bit?

That's something other than the lies your lips move to make

when you tell yourself you're fine, too.

I'm Over

Six feet tall

(--at least that's what I tell myself)

and

I'm Over

that last Super Bowl

(--because there's always next season, until there's not)

and

Of all the things I'm really really over

I'm Over

telling myself and at least everyone who asks

That yes,

I'm Over You.

I wrote four of these

In the time it took you

to finish that glass of wine

So here's to the next one

--I'll race you

Put it to your lips

before I put it to the page;

Both chasing this away in our own way

And I'll let you guess which is more self-destructive.

Patterns are for bad shirts

and my relationship behaviors, apparently

And thank you for giving it a shot anyways,

Three years of trying to save someone so clearly drowning

while treading water too

coming out (mostly) unscathed

maybe a little wet and out of breath

But much much

much

Better off

and a stronger swimmer with better fashion sense, too.

Losing you is the only thing worse

than watching Tom lose 'Bowls;

and I realize that references like *this*

date this a little bit,

But it's because we dated

a little bit

that these words are here in the first place, at all

So I'm getting older, like Tom, and it's sad

because I've only got a few big plays left in me, too

the losing likely to make the next play even more reckless

Than the reckless that initially attracted

and eventually lost

you.

I play with fire

the way you played with Barbie;

stole cars and hearts and big screen TVs

while you were stealing candy and
learning how to count

and you can count, blessings and more

that I'm the gone those items were

from the places I stole them;

the bad my tattoos told you

tracing them in my bed and for the first
time

my latest/greatest heist landed you there

back when the fire was from the candle
and the look in your eyes and only.

Gambling isn't good to me

But I'll bet I'm better

Than whoever is wasting all your time these days.

As if

Running out of time

isn't the most tragically romantic fun a breaking, slowly heart can have.

Yeah, you're the best I'll ever have

Drake before the come-up;

And I use future tense

Because I've already written the end

to this particular book;

So looking forward

to nights without you in them

is about all I have to look forward to,

and a hell of a lot more fun than looking back

Nights curled on couches

not half the fun now

Holding whiskey instead of

and waiting on mornings

Colder than May ought to be.

I don't miss the hair

Fucking everywhere in my apartment

after Fucking everywhere in my apartment;

And I'm still finding

Fucking hair

Everywhere

Silver strand ghosts

Hanging around and longer

Than you had sense to.

If *"Don't Let Me Push You Away"*

was the homework

then I failed you like that Grade 10 math

the first three times I took that driving test

and, I guess,

any hope in hell of being happy

the way you lied when you promised we could be.

Saudade

is my new favorite word and

well worth a Google;

it's the way I feel

about the distance I caused

too much time looking up weird words with meanings

I wouldn't need to worry about

if I'd just closed my book and paid attention.

Tell me

The things I lack;

Common sense

and

Self-Respect

and

Dignity

and

Everything you tell me

but the things you can't;

Penis size

and

Stamina

and

A voracious and all-consuming desire to consume you

Even after the things you tell me I lack

Running the way you should

and

Out of breath, too.

I'd rather

-skydive

-wrangle poisonous snakes

-visit my Grandmother

than move my lips to mouth

I'm sorry

the way I'm supposed to;

So here's everything but,

and for the behaviors

that pushed you out of the metaphorical planes

I'm left to consider jumping out of

legs willing to move when lips don't.

In your life

You're in love with a couple of things

and leaving

is one of them

and unfortunately for me

the other one won.

Today I almost threw out

The last of the things you bought for our old fridge;

Yeah, those make-them-yourself pickles were fucked

Until I saw how empty those shelves would be

And the whole "fend for myself" thing kicked up

And maybe I missed you

And so the preservatives-I-hope

Preserve;

Turns out the 'Best Before' date was on everything else.

In your defense

You thought 'Chinese Democracy' was worth the wait;

So even though you went from

This New One

to

That Old One

The memory of your musical taste

And your taste-taste

Earn you a page here on Volume Two

Way at the back, but still somewhat relevant

Like that band we listened to on days when the writing concerned you and only.

I thought about you once

While writing

Wrote about sunshine and summer days

And some other sappy shit

And then I thought about you a little more

tore that shit up

Wrote the pages with pretty bad pretty words in them

To maybe justify the fact I had to search my memory

For time with you I'll never spend

Present tense

And maybe a little bit because of the words I just wrote about you.

Interlude

I'm on store shelves

Alphabetical under 'Amazing'

Presenting better

Than the me you get to know

/deal with

And if a modicum of success

Has me insufferable

Imagine the nightmare time spent will be

When the book about you

Hits shelves beside books by lesser writers and better humans.

The Ones About Me (--and my epic and monumental shortcomings)

Of all the Irrational Animals,

Apologetic Alphas

are the fucking worst.

--so, sorry ;)

Inconsistently Awful

is amongst my favorite
of the names you called me;

Well-earned and spoken
more consistently
than the times I was
Consistently

Absent,

Emotionally and
finally,
Physically.

I write Volumes

so I don't have to speak them.

I've been writing more

And thinking less

About

And of

You

And the things that both push the pen

And out the door.

I'm worse on the weekend

which sucks for every Sunday

outside Football season

and for every girl

stupid enough to believe in sleepless Saturdays

or in me, at all.

So apologies for wasted ends

and worried weeks

knowing *next* is five or less away

and the whiskey or the season will stain me

the way last Sunday stained you.

I need Jesus

and church on Sunday

and a pretty big bath

if I'm gonna wash away the sins of someone else

staining my lips and my breath and the conscience beneath

the words that come out of my dirty mouth

when I tell you I'm not the sinner

my sins would so clearly beg to differ.

Just the right amount of

Despair and Determination

And I can write the kind of shit

To make your mother blush

And your daddy write me off

And if I practiced what I preach

I'd be the locked away I probably should be

Stealing futures unjaded

By horrible experiences with bad boys

Responsible for the jading

Since back when Oprah was fat

For the first time.

Irascible, but justifiably so.

I'll justify

Bad behavior and poor judgement

As job requirement

I'll call

Relentless stubbornness and an overwhelming desire to make my poorly-researched point

Necessary qualities for an introverted, introspective troubadour

And

I'm irascible

(--worth a google)

Because it makes the writing better

So when I call my bad behavior

Bones

And for my next book

Take it on the chin

Like the left I won't throw

Better at wounding with words

And childish temperament

Selfish and arrogant and petty and small

And (--thanks for buying this book!)

Celebrated for it.

Dressing pretty

Doesn't discount dirt
Hidden under nails and years

And

Poor

is just my judgement, now

Having fought hard to keep
"I'm from here"
the kind of secret I tend to,

--the kind that kills pretty, shows scars.

Motivation;

Backbeats

Bass Drums

&

Bad Words.

My Momma's Not Gonna Like This One

But fuck it, there's only about two pages that pass

Her rose-colored-glasses version of the son I'm not;

So once this sells

The way it should

I'm gonna buy a bobber

(Bonneville)

and a ball

(8)

and I'll either be super inspired

Or

super dead

By the time it's time for 139, 3.

I go for girls

with Sugar Baby Tendencies

Questionable asses and ethics

--like maybe real, maybe not

But the kind of girls I go for

are the kind of fun

that encourage the kinds of behavior

you're benefitting from, reading This Book

and the next one

about the next one

I swear

--this time for real!

that hurt me the hardest.

I'm on my Marcus Aurelius shit

Meditating

On the kinds of things a guy like me meditates on;

Thing like girls

And fights

And fights with girls

--the kinds of things

That pick up the pen

On days I'd rather not;

Write the things that my destroyed sense of self-worth would rather I didn't

--the kinds of things on the very next page.

I'm less about half-naked selfies

and more about half-naked soul-I-swear-I-still-have-one exposings;

and while my followers on the 'Gram might appreciate the former

You and a very small portion of the population

kinda digs the latent hopelessness of the latter.

So can we call these lyrics?

I've got too much testosterone for poems

Too much withering insecurity for free-verse

Too much false cleverness for anything remembering honesty

My Daddy isn't overly proud of me

and I kinda don't blame him

the sum of his son is several thousand fucks and the words surrounding them;

pages and pages to apologize for potential had and unrealized

brain damage and bad decisions where scholarships and sanctity used to/should be

before marriage/kids/settle became the bad words

and the bad words just became common.

I'm suicidal before coffee

and a little on Sundays

curmudgeonly earlier than I have any right to be

a rascal and a scoundrel and a bamboozler and a good person before six and only

The Patron Saint of Sometimes, still

and yet somehow I fall

into situations like this;

working hard to explain my lesser qualities

in the face of someone

foolish enough to stand in my wake

brave enough to hang around

long enough to prove myself right.

If my books are albums, then this shit is an EP

More punch per page, and these are the pages that punch back,

leaving me wounded and more exposed

than a book about some guy I pretend isn't me

I'll bury this one too, ten years done before advertised on sale

I'll blush when you bring it up, sign it different when you ask

Like I'm proud of it, I guess,

hide from it like the feelings

I tell myself aren't there

And then tell the world different when they read every single word after this one.

Friends and Family Members

Aren't crazy about this one

Like maybe I'm the kind of

Crazy

These pages kinda make me out to be

Or maybe I'm misunderstood

And it's one of those

As a Fox

jams;

Either way, I'm the topic of conversation

139 Pages should have painted you to be;

And I'll take it on the chin

Because the next one

--the one really about you?

Is 139 Pages away

From starting a whole new conversation.

138 Pages of Pining

Doesn't have quite the same kick

And so, while I swear this isn't just some half-assed attempt to pad the page count

You can't blame me

If the vein hasn't been tapped

And the blood it takes

(Of the sweat and tears too)

Isn't run dry

Running around

The troubled mind it takes

To pine for 138 Pages and............................

Last One

And I've got nothing clever left

So in closing

Just let me say

Thank You

For the hurt it took

To be this brave.

...139, 3.

aka the (probably) last volume of 139 Pages of Pining.

The Ones You're Likely Tired Of.

I ruined you

like the laundry that time

and you tell me
that time since

can't colour the memory
of time together

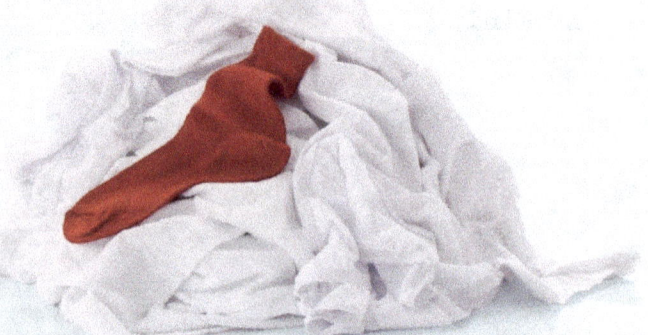

so while I'm sorry
for lesser years and pink-er
shirts

I promise you're not missing
much more than passive
aggressive passion

and an ungodly inability to
function independently.

...3

i sometimes sing

songs about someone else

everytime always
and
only

...except maybe this time

time took

my dog Dabber

and

the farm i grew up on

and

the last bit of hope i maybe sometimes almost had.

time took

that one sweater i liked

and

looking kinda good without filters

and

the reason why i write the way i do.

time took
the way dad threw a sprial

and

mornings without back pain

and

coffee being anything other than essential.

time took everything

but time

can't

touch

you.

Took four pills

The first told me to forget you

The second helped try real hard

The third went down with the whiskey

The fourth

--the fourth just justified the handful

I just justified

Swallowing, and removing that first 'S'

In the wake of slammed doors
And the nothing hiding behind them.

I write more in Leo Season

On what you'd call my self-indulgent indulgences

Like I lack the ability to rationalize the concepts you said I really should;

Concepts like

Together

and

Only

and for seasons decidedly longer than the season I leave you in

The Season attached to the traits that kinda sum up my leaving, and the self-indulgent reasons why.

I wrote this

2:38 on a Tuesday

and

you can guess which side of 12

inspired the kind of

inspired shit

2:38 and you

tends to create.

Downplay insecurity

with big bad words

and

Mask the hurt little boy

with scraped knuckles and tough talk

Hide the fact

that you're not who you intend to be

and

you tell yourself tomorrow and that bottle of whiskey

tonight

will make it anything close to okay.

I made this shit up on the go

on my "made this shit up on the go" shit

Rationalizing indignation and low-key barbarity

As creative expression

and

justified vengeance

and

all the minute rationalities

you and this fifth of vodka

made in your respective goings.

Where we come from is cold

...and that's no excuse.

There aren't enough Bon Iver albums
in the world

to make me any sadder

than the sad

your sullen silence

and my stubbed toes

(and maybe my manic self-diagnosed depression)

have left me and the dog
you left in your leaving.

Fuck Bon Iver.

I dare/hope

You fall in love with/find

Someone as fucked-up/fun

As me.

...3

I've got

Ten kinds of cancer

(--if the sick coming from my mouth is any indication)

Fucked up toenails

From walking coals to greener pastures

Hurting girls like you

and your best friend, too.

I'm all

Saccharine sadness

and

Sweet ignorance

Hunting hubris on the way

to rationalizing my intent for you

All the while

You're looking at me

With eyes bluer than any right to be

Hoping the water hiding behind

Isn't brought forth

By one of my more subtle Saturday nights.

Because I'm sad, Mom.

Save that gushy-love shit

for unresolved issues with

uncuddled kittens

and

curiously-cuddled Step-Fathers;

I'm on that

unrequited, undeniable

Eat-Your-Soul-Good-Luck-After

kinda
thing

--the kinda thing

This Thing

could kinda be.

Sentimentality

is for the weak

--this coming from the guy

closing in on 417 pages

of something dangerously close.

YOU JUST SAID SOMETHING DOESN'T ADD UP
BUT BEING GOOD WITH WORDS MEANS NOT SO MUCH WITH NUMBERS
LIKE THE 24 ANGRY WOMEN YOU REFERENCED IN YOUR RANT
OUTWEIGHS THE 8 BOOKS THE PAIN OF BEING A POET PROVIDED
AND THE 2 CAR GARAGE THE PAGES PROVIDED
ON THE WAY TO
THE ONE YOU SWORE YOU WERE
WHEN YOU SWORE YOU'D NEVER SWEAR AT ME
SOME 7 SWEARS AGO
NUMBERS ADDING UP FASTER THAN ACCUSATIONS
FROM 23 WOMEN I'M LOSING COUNT OF

...3

Your eyes have that kind of

'you should have kept paying my rent'

'you should have kept buying me expensive gifts'

'you should have booked that Mexico trip'

look in them,

and me and my

'I'm a starving writer I can barely feed myself'

honesty

honestly

is better served serving the

'you're the fucking man'

eyes your best friend is giving from the couch beside

you and your evil little eyes.

I wrote thirty-three pages (!)

that couldn't accurately describe

the thirty-three things

my imagination restrains me from

expressing to you.

So let this thirty-third page

serve as the warning

the first thirty-two really should have.

The Ones You Might Maybe Like.

You're more than

those big green eyes

and

that big fat ass

--and I swear, if you give me enough

volumes of 139

I'll come up with some way to tell you so.

You look like Jesus

probably

because Jesus isn't really real

and so maybe you kinda can't be, either

Smiling at me

with those Jesus teeth

and redeeming any hope I'd had

of dating you

without having to write a book about it.

Burning gas and validation

On my way to you

and your pedicured little toes

And they're not really suited

for the running away you really should

be running

And so we're towards

and the restaurant I fooled you into thinking

was anywhere near good enough

for the date we're about to go on

and the doom following desert.

Prince of Lies-To

(*too)

**come on, read slow.

Eyes like honey

Ass like

--like

--fuck, tried to think of something sweeter than honey

--so ass like *that*,

whatever is sweeter than honey.

WHISKEY

AND

COCAINE

AND

RAZOR-BLADES DANGEROUSLY CLOSE
TO WRISTS

BESIDE PENS DANGEROUSLY CLOSE
TO PAPERS

AND

YOU.   ...3

Yeah, to me *'Optimism' might be a four-letter word;*

But so is your name, "_ _ _ _"

and the sad part is that

–despite my admittedly immense vocabulary–

– –of all the nasty names I could call you/come up with to describe you

...fuck, you're still my favorite curse.

So, it turns out that you're not at the bottom of this particular bottle...

...good thing it's Wednesday, and I've got another try right here.

Despite how obnoxiously epic your eyes/ass is/are

the inconsistencies flowing from your lips can't/won't

make the metaphorical waves I'm swim/sinking

worth the occasional life-preserver

your smile/ass

(...and the occasional warm beverage/peace-offering...)

sometimes/honestly-always/but never again trick me into

Look, there's a chance I'm gonna lose the toe

I stubbed that time together

The one you swore I should get looked at but didn't

The way you swore I should have tended to you, too

but didn't

So, yeah, losing the toe's gonna hurt

but I'm blessed with nine more

and in nine since

I haven't found one

353

That swears quite like you.

ALL BURNED OUT ON BAD BEHAVIOUR
BUT FOR THE SAKE OF
PROSPERITY/CONSISTENCY/YOU

...I'LL LACE UP

FOR

ONE

MORE

ROUND.

I'm not scared of

Monsters under the bed

Ghosts in my head

or the prospect of ruining my integrity
by rhyming something about being dead

no

the only thing that scares me

is the thought of this being the page

you finally figure out

that all the other ones are about you

and this one makes you realize

you no longer care.

You were always my favorite word

that started with the letter 'L.'

and the loss I took

in the losing

of you and the ability to have fun with the words I used to

kinda makes the meaning of the ones that are left

--words and otherwise-

about as fun and meaningful as that time time took my dog Dabber.

(*So no fucking fun, at all.)

You and

Your perpetually pouty perfect little lips

and

the candied sweetness that falls from between them

tell me

and my baser tendencies

that, despite my resolution to leave

and leave perpetually unresolved

unrequitedness

you're not going anywhere

and

the part of me that thinks maybe this is all

just one really big CRY FOR HELP

really appreciates

you telling me.

PEANUT BUTTER AND JAM

SUNSHINE AND SUMMER DRESSES

BADLY BROKEN AND BRUISED EGOS

—THINGS THAT TASTE GREAT TOGETHER.

You're kinda fancy

Whiskey in a decanter

and all the subtle

of a Mack truck in a prayer circle

and

you've got me

praying

that you'll shine your not-so subtleties

on me.

Troubadour

Fighting Man

Fool.

Born with Mother's Devilment

and

Daddy's Eyes

Half-Gypsy Half-Rapscallion

Entirely

All

Yours

...if you can temper

Maltemper

and

Whiskey Lullabies.

...3

You're all

Static cling on freshly dried Sweaters

Powerlines humming on county roads

The kind of Charged-up crazy

Me and my over-stimulated synapses

Can really stick to.

*we're a match not just because the
adjectives start with the letter d*

but because you like me

despite all of the overwhelming evidence

that you really kinda shouldn't.

You're a mash up

of eating disorders and enthusiasm

and

me and my
All-Consuming Mental Health Issues

appreciate

the food-for-thought your comings and goings

have scrambled in the spot

reserved for reservations about Girls Like You.

you're all

Heat Lightning and High Tops

whether weather is
accommodating
(like you can be)

or

sullen
(like you kinda make me)

you're all

withering bombast

and

righteous indignation

and

i'm a sucker for it all

...because you're fucking
cute in Converse

I went twelve rounds with Chemistry

Flatlined Intervention

Beat Non-Verbal

But

Particles

Or

Connection

Or

Energy

—whatever the fuck it's called when something completely unwelcome overwhelmed us—

knocked my ass out

faster than Street Jesus with that flying knee.

...139, 3.

You've been on one

Since Bono could write a good song

Since backbeats and words-on-streets

Were lyrics and boom-bap boom-boom-baps

So

Forever long

On your pretty-hair-pretty-girl-pretty shit

Making mockeries of me

And the boys like,

Lost in songs better suited

To describe you and the girls like

On one

And then

On to the next one.

The Ones I'll regret by the time this comes out.

Seriously

put this on the shelf

beside the books that proclaim poetry and sell better

and

find one that even fucking remotely comes close.

How much more

'that much better'

can this be before

my book on the shelf

next to those lesser-than

reflects the patience and pain

I really only needed

1 or 2 pages

to kinda get the gist of.

I write more on road trips and bad days

and, for some reason,

Sundays

Devil's work on the Lord's day

Driving and Drinking

(coffee)

...well, if I'm honest, not just coffee

Because the whiskey bites harder on days without the burden of routine.

Where I come from

is about the only story I haven't told

and the tragedy of

the explanation/excuse it would give you

is every-only reason

it's the only story I won't tell.

This shit is so Next Level

this store needs a shelf ABOVE top shelf

for this shit to sit on.

This one is '139 Pages of Pining, Volume 3.'

(...but only because 'Manic Manifestations: Every Thought I've had about You Lately' would have an infinitely higher page count, and I'm tired/lazy as fuck.)

Maybe the Next One will be filled with some inspirational shit;

All "You're worth it, sister" (and other manipulations.)

So there's blood in my urine

and the doc swears it's not from the metaphorical blows

your literal leaving

has left me;

and the prescription is not

the whiskey and commiseration

my procrastination prefers;

running out of clever words and the closeted comforts

my constant peeing reminds me

were never really comforts at all.

Mr. Missed the Mark,

The Patron Saint of Almost-Maybe

like

'almost-maybe took advantage of those scholarships'

'almost-maybe won that Breakthrough Novel Award'

'almost-maybe kept the anybody that inspired either this book, or one just like it;'

instead it's

the latest volume of the series that won't make me famous

written about the latest girl who's better off anywhere but the

Stuck

she most certainly is

hanging on to Mr. Missed the Mark

and his ever-increasing volumes of increasingly less quiet rants of not-quite-quiet desperation.

I wrote

The One That Could Change My Life

In my sleep last night;

The sleep I woke from

And let the weight of waking in the world I wake to

Keep me from both writing it down

And remembering to remember it.

I'm ten kinds of crazy

--or at least ten women have told me so

But if they're at least a little crazy too
Do I let their respective diagnoses
Distract me from the kinda-glaring fact

That my ten kinds of crazy
Kinda created the book you're holding
And reading about the kinda crazy

At least ten women leaving has left me?

Mitigate your remembrance of our time together

Mediate your rationalizations of why

Temper your reaction to mine

and

Marvel at my daedal ability to throw it all away.

The dichotomy being that I either really care, or really don't.

Maybe the next one will be '139 Pages of Positivity.'

-because it's only up from here

...right?

I came up with ten pages

to describe The Top Ten

Things I Haven't Told You!

ten in light of

the ten-thousand-thousand

that I have;

and all I could come up with

by the top of page ten

was that I'm not really equipped

to talk about ten

or any number, really, other than

that one thing I did tell you

that left a hole big enough

for ten hypothetical pages

and one badly broken boy

to try to fill.

How fucking cool are

-Sunsets

-French Bulldog Puppies

-Whiskey no-chasers

And

How fucking cool are
All of the above

when

The Reason for appreciating them

stops appreciating you.

Horribly Self-Centered, yeah

But the kind that

comes up the with kind of content

that only victims of Horribly Self-Centered creative cunts

can really dig.

*(So, you're welcome.)

This has to be like 80

so we're in the home stretch;

just under 50 pages of

perpetual whining

before I close the book

on my books of somewhat celebrated

calculated discontent...

...but who's counting?

Raggedy

Rough

Wild

Five degrees left of where I
should have been

Somehow right where mom and
dad and the cop that time
told me I'd end up.

Irascible and no further
ahead

Than the behind I left

Every Anyone who tried to
make it different.

The Ones I Can't Fit into Other Categories.

All of this is exhausting

And not the kind of exhausting

It was when I started,

18 years

and

8 books
and
The optimism of 18 years ago.

No, now it's the kind

Of dragged-down-to-the-marrow

Mined-the-depths-of-my-soul

18 years older

Exhausting...

The kind of exhausting

I'm gonna need

3 baths

and

10 sleeps

and

18 years

to recover-if-recovering-is-recoverable-at-all

from.

I took a break from

my self-righteous self-destruction

to try you and

your cute little eternal optimism

on for size;

and the truth is

while I appreciate your joie de vivre

my audience and the audience in my head

prefer the trappings of

feeling perpetually trapped.

*And the grand-total of my labors, laid out
oh-so-laboriously before you*

Is roughly 575, 345 and counting

Words rationalizing

Why there are no words.

...no wonder I'm so fucking tired.

Table your transgressions

And

Bottle your barbarity;

It's Whiskey Tuesday

And

No amount of razor-tongued retributions

Can top the

Delicious damage

Me and my boy Jack are about to

Self-Inflict tonight.

Exercise and Exorcise

Body and the Demons

That honestly kinda took over

And

Maybe one or two more

Bench/pull ups before

The pressing issues

Work themselves out;

Satan in the sweat

And

Devil in the details

Take

Time

And

Take

Care

And

Take the parts of me

I lied when I promised you

Were unavailable

The way I most certainly

/emotionally

Am.

Take

That.

You kinda killed

pizza on Fridays

nerve endings on fingers

Fun

When you went the way you went

So

Away

Leaving me and that couch you said you loved

Alone

And for Falls

Since

That fall you made me.

...3

This is on some island/summer breeze shit

Wavy and Breezy and

Light

Like the one you're likely reading this under.

Yes, my parents are disappointed in me

And

Yes, I'm guilty of everything you've accused me of.

Yes, I'm responsible for the myriad of emotions on these pages

And

The saccharine sadness of the girls I wrote them for.

Yes, I'm a morally bankrupt (almost) 40-year-old degenerate

And

No, there's nothing you and your savior complex can do about it.

--but you're more than welcome to try.

Today's Sobering Cold Comfort:

Time

Takes

The

Talentless

,too.

Crushingly Insensitive.

(...and yet, oddly, Overwhelmingly Expressive.)

I wrote a book about me.

I wrote a book about her.

I wrote a book about nothing and no one in particular.

I wrote a kid's book about dogs, even.

I wrote book after book

And I told myself they were about anything other than

What they're only and obviously all about

...I wrote nine books about you.

"It'll be better in the long run"

& other lies you tell yourself.

"Write one about me,"

You said

Pretending as though you didn't know

All that I've ever really written

And all that I never will

Is really all about you anyways.

You're determined

and

I'm despondent

And

I guess that's why this kinda works.

I SEE GHOSTS

WITH NAMES LIKE TINKY AND MICA AND SOUSA

AND

ALL THE CUTE LITTLE NAMES I CALLED YOU

BACK WHEN YOU WEREN'T A GHOST

YET

AND READING ABOUT OTHER

GHOSTS

WITH CUTE LITTLE NAMES

SOMEHOW TRICKED YOU INTO BELIEVING

YOU WOULDN'T HAUNT ME, TOO.

...3

Do you remember the time

I was more the amount of unobtained potential

and

I was less the sum of unrecognized greatness?

Me either.

18 years of writing and I've learned

There's no famous overnight

There's no famous, at all

There's no at all, at all

either

...there's just the resignation that

Writing to make the pain less,

is just going to have to be more than enough.

Older

Just kinda means

Desperate, more

...not the wiser, I was really counting on

Counting years

and wondering why relevance

didn't follow that first grey hair.

"Easy to Read!"

and

"A couple pretty pictures!"

and

more smoke and mirrors to distract

from the very serious mental health-related ruminations

ruminating on the rest of these pages.

I ran out of clever

About 139 pages ago

so for the next 33

expect more of the same;

Moaning about the women smart enough to run away

And the words written hastily/stupidly

to make them.

416

The Ones I hope are Kinda Clever.

You wear 'Hard to Get' like your favorite sweater,

the one I plan on stealing

slowly and methodically

chipping away at whatever resistance

you admirably had

and likely lost

like that oversized hat

I suddenly look so damn good in.

You put the gravel in my guts

The pen in my hand

The end to this book

I'm writing right after

I deal with the damage

Not dealing with you until

Right now

Has me dealing

And not especially well with.

You always hated

that I ran hotter

like body-heat and my inability

to let you fuck with my thermostat

fucked with your ability

to let you fucking live with me.

Here it is, the Latest and Greatest Thing I'm Sad About

Ruthlessly edited

Chopped and Screwed

Finished

The way I really and truly am;

Until you or The Next One

Causes The Next One.

WILDLY ERRATIC
AND WILDLY INCONSISTENT
AND REALLY JUST WILD.
AND THE ____EST PART
IS MY WOEFULLY INEPT INABILITY
TO RETURN THE BETTER PARTS OF YOUR WORST TENDENCIES
WITH ANYTHING OTHER THAN OVERLY AGGRESSIVE INTEREST.

I'm like Trip Fontaine

One really douchey name away

from the confidence it kinda takes

to take down the kinda girls

that inspired

the book in your hands

the name in the feels

the thanks my momma gave

to The God there isn't

when she settled on Brody Drew;

the (slightly) less douchey name

she settled on

so that I never would.

(Settle...read again.)

Don't worry, *I hurt myself* so you won't have to.

Kk I'm a fully confident super sexed-up Superman;

but you're on the kind of 12/10 shit

that makes me question every questionable fashion choice I've ever made;

like I'm punching way above my weight class

and swimming two oceans deep

looking into whatever water colored those eyes

sitting across tables that might as well be deserts

Here at the dinner you're way too good for

So order all the deserts

because you deserve at least everything o the menu

and I'm hoping the hole burning in my wallet

makes up for the misplaced hair I'm
suddenly sure

your confidence shattering beauty

has stunned straight

like all the hair

standing suddenly at attention

on the back of the neck

I'd pay anything to have your little hand
around.

Climbing over clichés

On the way to you and that better-than-store-bought ass

And my Grade 10 English Teacher

is gonna be disappointed in this one too;

But I'm running out of the clever it takes to come up with new ways to tell you

I'd really like to.

*How many more Really Fucking Clever
poems before I can pull off a fedora?*

Remember all the times

I'd let you drive

and write from shotgun

like the inescapable fear of impending death

your little lane changes induced

inspired the pages

you've

(so far)

Lived to read.

Springfield, Ontario

isn't really even on the map

but I really feel like

a couple more of these collections

and

'Home of Brody Drew'

isn't the kind of unreasonable

the rest of This reads like.

The kind of not confident

Botox and Whiskey

kinda can't cover

and in the posing for the

cover

of This Very Collection,

I'm thinking it's gonna take

more than fillers and filters

to recover from the damage

You and 40 years of negligent skincare routines

scratched into the skin

of the not-white-enough teeth I'm hanging on by.

You're warm and cozy,

Asbestos in Grandma's basement

and the parts of you I can't repulse with less-than-flattering descriptions

really kinda digs

the holes I do

(Dig)

Every. Time. I pick up this pen.

Fuck You, do better.

I mean, I've still got it

but it's a little harder to keep these days;

Everything hurts a little more than it used to

(and not just the type of shit you'd assume hurts when you read the rest of this)

No

I mean the back and the shoulder

and

the rest of the shit that keeps me awake

tossing and turning

when the tossing and turning

gets tired of being all about you and the girls like

when the sobering reality that my days of charming you and the rest

with candied words and the rest of the package

my admittedly impressive package presents

goes the way of my back

before that one deadlift

that made my admittedly impressive package just a little less so;

when nights became more about tossing and turning

and less about wrestling and writhing

you and the girls like.

I'm terrified of planes

(and more accurately, turbulence on planes)

so I guess that means I'm terrified of crashing

and

into you

counts as crashing

and so I guess I'm terrified of counting, too

and terrified of what it all means;

crashing into you and dealing with the wake of

the potential of not waking

and not seeing you again

the way this next flight kinda means I might not.

Running out of pages to write on

words to express

ways I can/can't feel

and the women it took

the cumulation of 3 volumes to tell

myself and anyone who will read this

...I'm really sorry for almost all of it.

I remember thinking there was so much more

road to run on

stories to tell

people to hurt and escape the weight of it

--time.

And now that there's not

I can't help but think

maybe there's just enough

to realize I never really had any at all.

Confuse contemplation for commiseration

and

alliterations

like

the cold you cause in your callous conniving

for insight into my admittedly troubled mind

and reflections on your decidedly dark worldview

--either way

When it comes to reading me from the pages I wrote here for you to read

you're as wrong

as your momma told you we were for each other

that very first time she told you

and you didn't listen

because you don't

because the callous conniving manipulative-minded machinations

amongst my diagnosed alliterations

couldn't confuse well worded warnings

for genuine care.

This is the home stretch

for tired feet and well-worn worry

and I do

worry

that the miles travelled

in the stories told

have left paths beaten and broken

on roadsides intended

for spouted flowers and unbridled optimisms.

I can't remember

Who won the game last Sunday

who left me two before you did

who starred in that movie

I forgot we both liked.

I can't remember

the weather that December

that caused the blanket-drowned confessions

that caused this book.

I can't remember

why it hurt so bad

I picked up a pen

instead of the phone...

All I remember

All these years later

is that I knew you'd cause all of this

...and that your inevitable return

will cause that much more.

See you soon.

Thank you to every

one

who inspired every

word.

For the sake of both chronicling and your peace of mind, the following women contributed to the three volumes of '139 Pages of Pining'

....

You

And

You

And

You

And

You

And

Yes, you

And

You

And

Especially most certainly

...you.

Promotion

aka 'pictures I used to attempt to convey the overwhelming sarcasm the books entail.'

You're Double-Stuffed
Oreos

to my inner fat kid;

90 mile-per-hour run from
the cops

to my socially-
challenged/misunderstood
mid-twenties

Heroin

to my just-wait-till-I'm-
successful indulgences

Yeah, I guess this is my
way of saying

You're pretty

And I think you're pretty
cool.

139, 2.

Dressing pretty

Doesn't discount dirt
Hidden under nails and years

And

Poor

Is just my judgement, now

Having fought hard to keep

"i'm from here"

The kind of secret i tend to

—the kind that kills pretty, shows scars.

139, 2.

Apologetic Alphas

are the fucking worst

—so, sorry ;)

139, 2.

For such a cute voice

you sure make hurtful sounds.

139, 2.

The Realest Shit I've Ever Wrote

is the shit I've yet to write about you.

...139, 2.

Headstrong & Half-Hearted & Full of Great Ideas.

...3

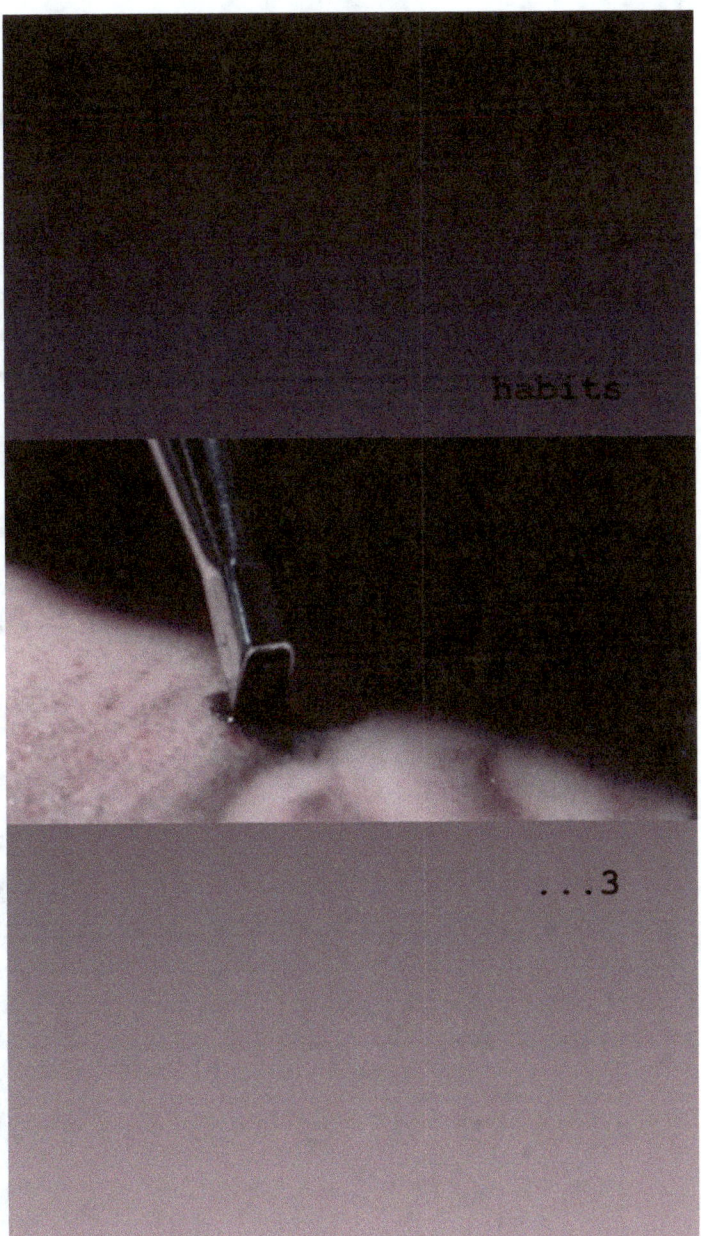

habits

...3

only always.

...3

last rodeo

...3

blowing up relationships like

...3

delivering heat

about the girls.
for the 'bois.

...3

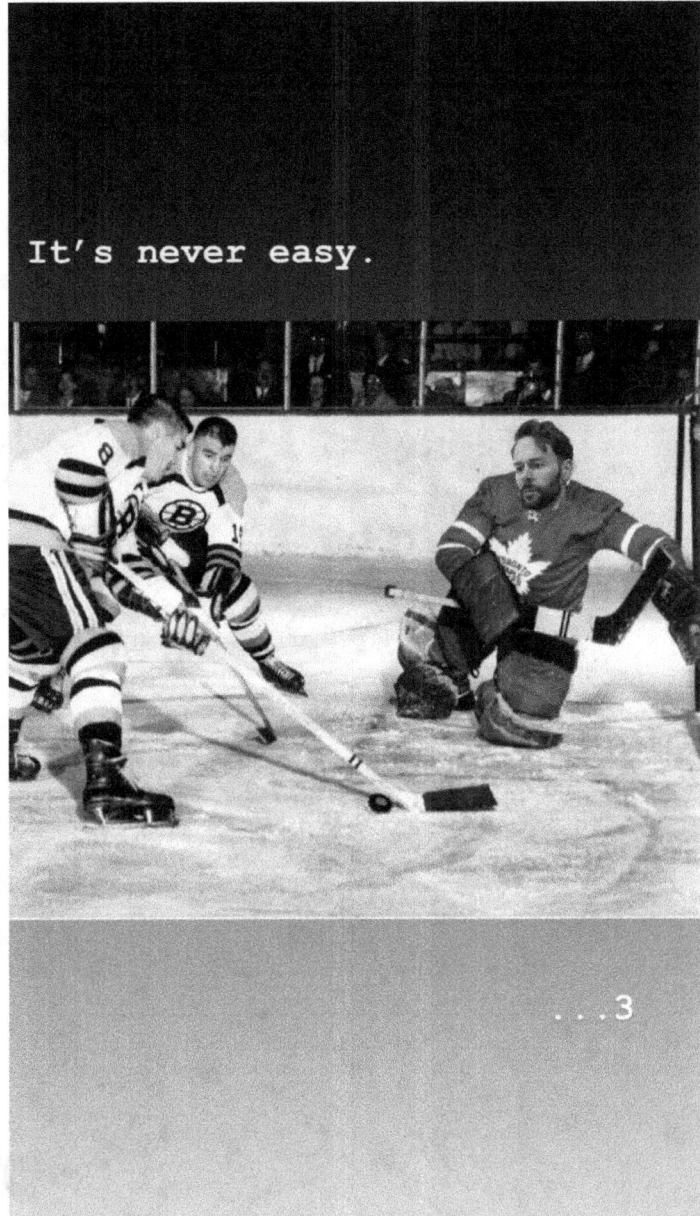

real quick.

...3

mellow

...3

worse on weekends and waxing moons

...3

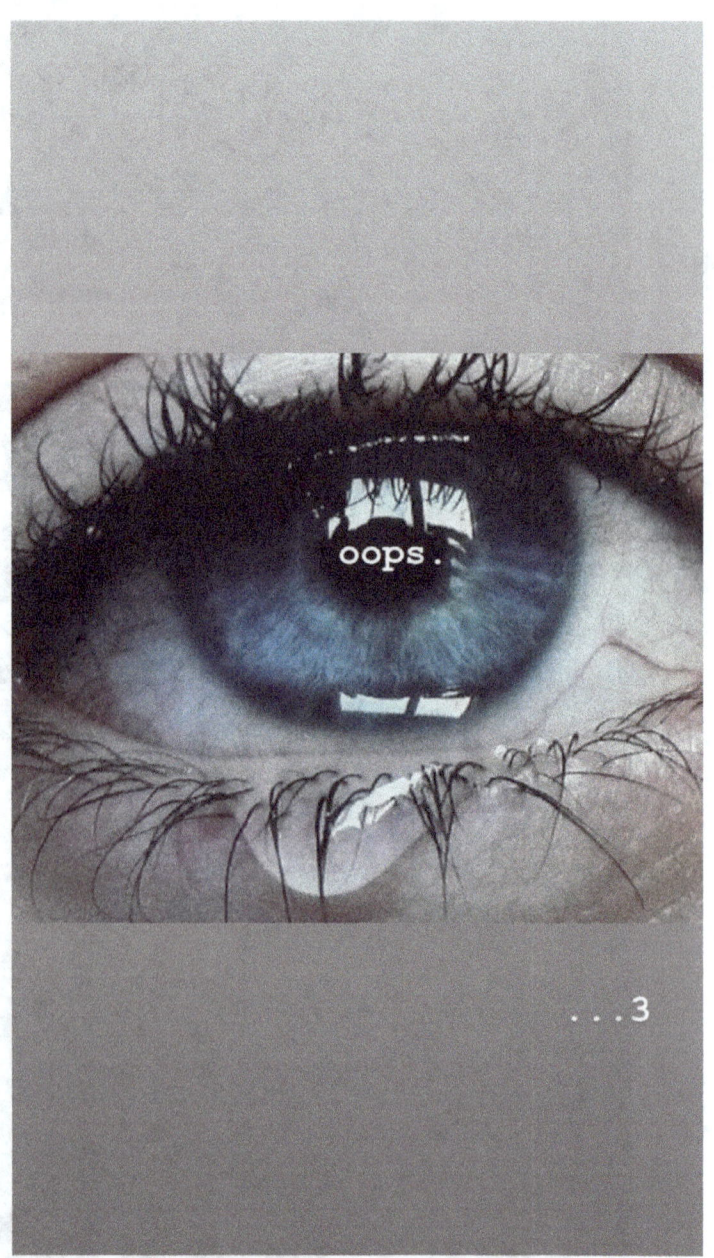

mas brusco

...3

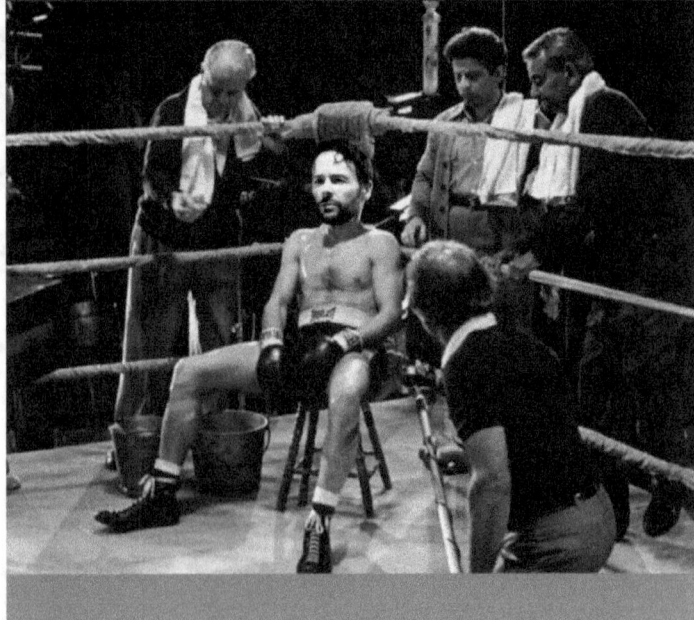

it's about time.

...3

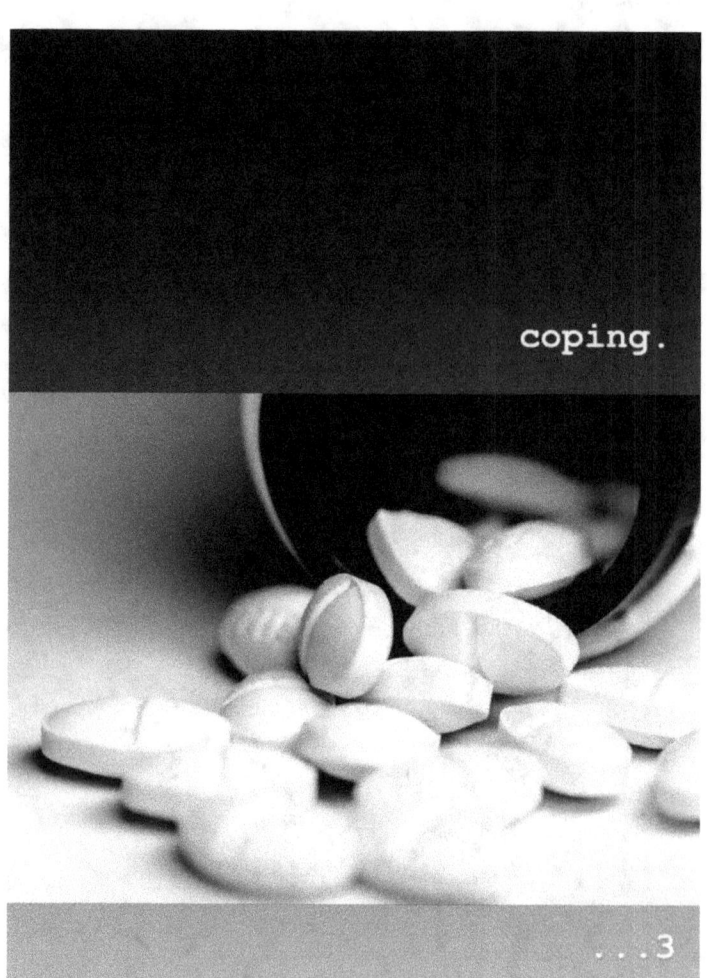

coping.

...3

Winging it.

dropping tracks.

...3

pushing boundaries.

...3

half-calculated chicanery

...3

www.ingramcontent.com/pod-product-compliance
Lightning Source LLC
Chambersburg PA
CBHW070041120526
44589CB00035B/2019